MOON

A MELODY FOR MY LUNA

BARATH PRIYAN

She conquered My Heart
just like the Moon
conquered the Sky.

As a sky let me hold my
Moon in my hands and
show My World till the
end.

Just like a Half Moon bright up the World in Peace and Happiness, she bright up my world with her Eternal smile.

Healing Myself with the
Feeling of yourself under
the Moonlight with
some Melody in the air.

Somehow I am Tangled
with Her Heart even
though she is apart
Waiting with the wound
of a part with the sound
of my Heart.

Instead of Falling in her Words of Thorns I rather die in her Caring arms.

I love you till my last
Breathe that leads to my
First Death...in the scent
of the Moonlight.

A love like yours comes
once in a Blue Moon and
let me be a Stupid man
to Treasure it.

Your Love is More
Dazzling than the Stars,
more Charming than the
Full Moon, and Brighter
than the Sun.

When I told about you
to the Moon She just
Blushed and Light up the
Whole Sky all night.

Hey my Luna
Let me Hold you in
Hands and Treasure it by
my Love.
All My Poems are not
Enough to tell about
Her
She's everything.

Even a Million Copies of
Paper won't be Enough
to Write my Million
Feelings for Her.
Her love and care is
Priceless Just like the
Moon.

Looking for you in every
Lightyear
To get that word to
become a pair
I will be waiting for you
Until that word come
from you
Cuz I will Love you till
the Limit with the Most
Precious Heart of mine.

The smell of love
A Fragrance of Her
Spreaded in Air
My eyes paused
The moment was touché
in the Heart
Where I was able to Hear
the sound of My Heart
By the Wound in the Part
of My Heart.

When I wake up
She's on my mind
When I go to sleep
She's on my mind
From the morning
Till the night
Where every second I
melt.
Why not? Some people
are worth melting for.

I truly think it's my boon
To have her care
To have her love
To have her presence.....
Just no words in the
whole universe to
describe that feel for her
It's just
" Tu Me Manques".

I made a melody with my
love for you
But when I played it my
guitar gone broken
Where as no instrument
can play my pure love
In which it can be heard
by you and I.

At looking your eyes in
Moonlight
Once again my Feeling
ignite.

Even her Blush is
Blushed by the Blush of
Her that bright up the
World.

In the smell of love
through the air
She just carried me with
her care
Once again I stunned
and
I didn't utter a word to
her
But I just carried her
with my love.

I was able to see her
Even in the sea of people
That was our love.

My eyes strained
As there was a light as
bright as moonlight.
Where my pearl looked
like a pearly moon where
she was my light in the
dark
As I still loved her where
she cared me as light.

It was a dark ocean
I dived
In a search of a pearl
Where it was cold
As my heart was frozen
With an eternal emotion
To see the light
To see her.

It remainder me of her
presence
While I was struggling in
her absence
Though it was a half
moon
It smiled at looking at me
It was far...
I really missed her.

I always wanna be with
you
No one can be like
You
She's my butterfly girl
Who always fluttering in
my heart.

Remembering you
Somehow give me bliss
Definitely
It will be eternal I guess.

One day
I wondered why the
moon was angry
As it was red
Then I found that
It saw my world moon
talking with me
Who was Prettier than
her.

I guess
I am missing someone
badly
In the sky
Don't know it maybe
It may not be.

Talking to the moon
Under the moonlight
Searching everywhere
But the direction is lost
Even though walking in
traces of my heart.

My book of life ended
But your love writes the
sequels.

I will be still there for
you just like a seconds
hand for minutes hand
in clock lets live together
with time.

It's not about the readers
who give worth to my
poems
It's just your love that
will be worth to my love
When you are gone
The poems are buried in
the air.

I call her my highness
Who conquered my
kingdom in my heart
I call her my moon who
conquered my everything
in my world.

I just miss her
Like sun misses the
moon
In daytime
It will never happen
But waiting for the
eclipse
To see her atleast once
again.

When I opened my pen
to see the ink
Cuz I kept writing
poems for a longtime
Though the ink was over
It kept writing about her
Yeah that's I don't need
ink
I just need my heart my

feelings for her to write
it.

I remember my moon
when she blushed and
hidden yourself in the
sky by reading my
poems.

Hey my Moon
Do you wanna know
How much I love you
Just see the sky beyond
you where it ends.

I use to set every evening
She use to rise every
night
We both loved eachother
Just as far as we are
But our heart are with
eachother.

She made the world
So cold at night...
The weather was so
pleasant
As a fallen leaf still
I constantly weathering
with her
Under the moonlight.

Don't be among a stars
for the Moon
For her
Just be like a brightest
star
For her
Just like a sun
For the Moon.

It's gift to get someone
Just like the moon
It's a eternal happiness
To talk to her
It's a boon
To show her your love
When she gives it back

It's a true meaning of a
life
To treasure it with my
pure love
Even when it is happy.
Even when it is sad
I always go to the moon
I go to her
I go to home.

Even when we are far
away
Just remember
We are just like letters
U and I in the keyboard
We are always together
By the soul.

I really wondered
When I kept writing
about her for years
Then I realised
She was my everything
In my heart
It's hard to write

everything
But It's happy to treasure
my everything.

On that day
The moon didn't appear
But I was still able to see
her
Just when I looked your
eyes.

I love to hold her in my
hands
Just like the sky holds the
Moon in his hands.

She was the one who
gave her shoulders when
I was sad
She was one I call her
highness
She was one I call her my
sweet little mom

Till my last breathe stays
Let my words admire
her.

Under the deep sea
We see the brighest jewel
a pearl
Up the high sky
We see the brighest star
A Moon
But with me I see her

My pearl moon.

I see her as a only rose
In my garden
That light-up everything
Just like a only moon
In the sky
That light-up the whole
world.

Even when she is far away
Somehow we are tangled
Together in our hearts
By these soulful poems.

Whenever it is lonely
Just call her
Just call the moon
You'll see your home
You'll see your little mom
You'll see everything.

Hey my Luna
She gave me the melody
She gave me the chord
She gave me the rhythm
But my song gone
incomplete
Without her love.

I kept looking at my
phone
for your text
Just like I kept looking
the sky for my moon
Missing her a lot.

I admire my love just like
I admire my moon my
Luna my girl.

She was my melody
I needed her to fulfill my
song
It's just a sound
without my music
Without her love
Without our feelings.

I kept looking at the
empty sky for the Moon
Just like I kept looking
for her in the no man's
land.

Those million words
can't describe my love for
her
Just like the million stars
can't be bright as moon
Just like a million hearts
Can't hold my love for

her.

Not all the songs are
relatable to her
There are some songs
Which can be heard by
just YOU and I
Under the moonlight.

I wanna close eyes
Just don't wanna see
tomorrow
To reach sky high with
my sorrows
In the memories of her
Let me die in the hands

of my Moon
Atleast with a smile.

To see the best version
Of the caring Moon
Just look at her eyeballs
you'll see your love
you'll see her.

Everywhere in the air
I was able to hear her
Voice
Calling me with the scent
of Moonlight
To play that melodic
musical chord.

I love her till and beyond
the Moon till the end of
the light-years.

Hey my Luna
Let us hold our hands
Sail under the clouds
Dive into the sky
Let's reach her
Let's reach our home
Let's reach the Moon.

Even when she is far away
But she always takes
place in my eyes
In my heart too.

When she light up the
sky
Up all night
Once again my eyes and
My feelings ignite.

It was like a stormy cloud
It's just a empty Dark sky
She wasn't there
Even it was dark in my
eyes
Started to miss her..
Waited for the day

When she comes back to
me
When she comes back
home.

Moon
She was the highness in
the sky
She was the highness in
my heart too
She lights up everything..
Even this book.

Remembering her voice
When you are alone
Remembering her care
When you are sad
Remembering her
presence
On her absence

Remembering her smile
Juz remembering her.

www.ingramcontent.com/pod-product-compliance
Lightning Source LLC
LaVergne TN
LVHW090132160826
845673LV00017B/2445
* 9 7 9 8 8 9 1 3 3 4 7 2 4 *